Heads and Tales

Stories of the Sages to Enlighten Our Minds

With Translation and Commentary
By Edwin C. Goldberg

UAHC PRESS
NEW YORK, NEW YORK

Library of Congress Cataloging-in-Publication Data

Talmud. Selections.
   Heads and tales : stories of the sages to enlighten our minds / with translation and
commentary by Edwin C. Goldberg.
      p. cm.
   Nine brief tales, most from the Talmud, in vocalized Hebrew with English translation
and commentary.
   ISBN 0-8074-0797-6 (pbk. : alk. paper)
   1. Legends, Jewish. 2. Talmud--Legends. 3. Midrash--Legends. I. Goldberg, Edwin C.
II. Talmud. English. Selections. III. Title.

BM530 .T352 2002
296.1'276--dc21
                                                                        2002071971

Designer: Shaul Akri
Typesetting: El Ot Ltd., Tel Aviv
This book is printed on acid-free paper
Copyright © 2002 by UAHC Press
Manufactured in the United States of America
10 9 8 7 6 5 4 3 2 1

This book is dedicated to the memory of my father, Wesley Goldberg, ל"ז, who loved a good story and was a man of high principles.

CONTENTS

PREFACE

The ancient Jewish Sages who composed the Talmud and Midrash were known for their expertise. Jewish law was their focus. Nevertheless, there also exists in this literature numerous narrative portions, examples of very short stories worthy of modern literary standards. A close reading of these stories offers both meaningful lessons for life and an appreciation for the artistry of these ancient teachers. One might even compare these "miniature" stories to haiku poetry because, like haiku, these tales often appear at first glance to be quite simple, but a careful study of them affords great insights into human nature in general and into our own struggle with spiritual challenges in particular.

The goal of this book is to assist the reader in understanding the profound simplicity contained in these stories. As the name of this book implies, these are stories for the "head"—that is, the mind. Their lessons can help us become more aware of our own human limitations and challenges, even as such stories reflect the ancient Sages' own wary views of humanity. And yet they are also *stories* and therefore they seek to engage our emotions as well as our minds. These stories entertain as they educate.

As we will see, the Sages who composed the Talmud and Midrash, and who often held the title "rabbi," did not avoid seeing in themselves the imperfections and hypocrisies found in other less religious people. Indeed, a striking characteristic of this literature is the willingness of the Sages to be critical of themselves.

Nine stories from the Midrash and the Talmud are presented in this collection. Following each story there is an essay designed to help the reader establish a method of closely "deciphering" the message of the story and understand how the story is written. Questions are also provided. Ideally, these questions and insights can be used to foster a discussion with other people concerning the stories. Traditionally Jews study with at least one other person in order to help glean from the material as many insights as possible. In Hebrew this is known as chevruta, and it remains a wonderful way to read a text.

Before presenting the stories there is a short introduction to the discipline of close reading. This technique is, of course, not limited to ancient Jewish stories, but utilizing this method will enable the insights of the short stories in the volume to be offered up to the reader.

Like the stories themselves, this book is short; but also like them, it is worthwhile to read each chapter slowly and carefully. In our modern world we rarely read this way, yet there is an advantage to such an approach. Reading slowly, we can savor the effective use of dialogue, narrative, and tone to present the lessons offered by the storyteller. We can enjoy the pleasures of reading for the sake of reading, instead of as a means to an end. And we can allow our imaginations to mull over the ethical dilemma implicit in the stories. For in this harried world, sometimes nothing is better than a good, well-written tale.

Acknowledgments

I am grateful to the Melton Centre for Jewish Education in the Diaspora of the Hebrew University for providing me with the opportunity to study with Jonah Fraenkel and Jonathan Cohen. Their insights into the creativity of rabbinic short stories, as well as the comments of Yair Barkai, have made possible this work. Many thanks also to the congregants of Temple Israel of Hollywood in Los Angeles and Temple Judea of Coral Gables, Florida, for granting me the opportunity to teach this material. I am grateful as well to the Florence Melton Mini-School in Miami and the University of Judaism in Los Angeles for similar opportunities.

I also want to thank Ken Gesser, the publisher, for suggesting that I write this book, and Rabbi Hara Person for her great help in its preparation. I would like to thank the rest of the UAHC Press staff who helped prepare this book for publication, including Stuart Benick, Rick Abrams, Liane Broido, and Bryna Fischer. Finally, I am extremely grateful for the guidance and support of my wife, Melanie Cole Goldberg, and for the continued inspiration of my children, Joseph and Benjamin.

INTRODUCTION
THE ART OF CAREFUL READING

When we read a selection from the Talmud, the corpus of Jewish law and story from fifteen hundred years ago, or from the Midrash, the commentary on the Bible from the same period, it is important to know the background of the material. In other words, readers with some Jewish education will know something of the Jewish communities of Palestine and Babylon. Readers should also have some general knowledge of how the Jewish community operated at the time. For example, we might ask, "What authority did the Sages have, and who were the most revered leaders?" We might ponder how these stories were taught and why they were told in the form they are presented in. These contextual concerns help us appreciate the significance of the teachings.

Nevertheless, when it comes to interpreting the miniature stories presented in this collection, a different discipline is helpful. According to this approach, we read the stories as a closed system, one in which the extraneous issues are barely considered. We assume that the writer of the story offers us a tale that needs no more information than what is provided. In other words, when reading a story concerning Rabbi Akiva, we need not know much about Rabbi Akiva to appreciate the lesson of the story. Scholars call this approach the "hermeneutic principle," which means that we can interpret the story based on what we have in front of us alone. Moreover, if the story is well written, there is often an internal symmetry: the beginning of the story reflects the ending and vice versa. A careful reader can even break the story down into various well-balanced parts. And in comparing these various parts we can learn about the message of the story itself.

For example, consider the following miniature story:

1 רַב שִׁימִי בַּר אָשֵׁי הָיָה מָצוּי לִפְנֵי רַב פָּפָּא וְהָיָה מַקְשֶׁה לוֹ הַרְבֵּה.

2 יוֹם אֶחָד מְצָאוֹ נוֹפֵל עַל פָּנָיו וְשָׁמְעוֹ וְאוֹמֵר: הָרַחֲמָן יַצִּילֵנוּ מִבּוּשָׁה שֶׁל שִׁימִי.

3 קִיבֵּל עָלָיו שְׁתִיקָה וְשׁוּב לֹא הִקְשָׁה.

1 Rav Shimi bar [son of] Ashi was a student under Rav Papa. He would constantly ask him [Rav Papa] difficult questions.

2 One day he [Rav Shimi] overheard [Rav Papa] praying to himself: "May the Merciful One save me from the disgrace of Shimi."

3 At that instant he [Rav Shimi] resolved to be silent and not trouble him with questions anymore.

This tale, from the Babylonian Talmud tractate *Taanit* 9b, is one that might strike a chord for a modern teacher. Every teacher has had a student who asked many difficult questions.

As in the story, the motivation for the questions is often not clear. Perhaps the questions reflected a desire to learn more. Perhaps they reflected an underlying suspicion about the ability of the teacher. Or maybe they are indicative of an insecure student trying to dominate the conversation.

When reading this short tale, many readers would give it a glance, come to a quick conclusion regarding "what it's about," and then go on to something else. The traditional Jewish model, however, teaches us to read the story carefully with a *chevruta* partner. The story would be analyzed from many perspectives. For example, what might have been Shimi's motivations? How did Papa choose to understand Shimi's actions? How did Shimi choose to understand Papa's words?

A sample list of questions that could be discussed might include the following:

1. What are the possible motivations for Rav Shimi's constant asking of difficult questions?

2. How long have the interchanges between Rav Shimi and his teacher been going on?

3. Why doesn't Rav Papa confront his student directly?

4. What are possible interpretations for the "disgrace *(boosha)* of Shimi"?

5. How does Rav Shimi choose to interpret Rav Papa's prayer?

6. Did Rav Papa mean for Rav Shimi to overhear the prayer? Why was Shimi listening?

7. Why does Rav Shimi stop asking questions?

In addition to these questions concerning the content of the story, another important issue is the *form* of the story. In other words, does the story itself—that is, its language and structure—help us in understanding the meaning of the story?

The purpose of asking so many questions of a miniature story is to foster a greater awareness of the tale's possible meanings. Upon sustained reflection it becomes clear that the story is more complicated than an initial reading would suggest. For instance, is Shimi's behavior characteristic of the ubiquitous class pest, or do his questions reflect a more noble goal, that of enriching the discussion? Furthermore, does the "disgrace of Shimi" refer to the student's embarrassing the teacher or to Shimi's own foolish position, which the teacher and the other students recognize even if Shimi himself does not?

A sustained study of the story should also lead the reader to appreciate the form of the story. A careful reading shows how the form mirrors the content: just as the motivations behind the characters' actions are far from clear, so, too, the text itself is laconic and ambiguous. Far from being an example of poor writing, the cryptic language reflects the difficulty inherent in interpreting the actions and words of others without a direct confrontation. The reader is in the dark, but so are the characters! The tale is also well balanced, with each one of the three parts being of similar importance in the story.

So much for the tale, but what about the head? How does this story help us gain a greater appreciation of our human foibles? Clearly the message is relevant and challenging: often we react to the actions and words of others without stopping to understand the actual motivations behind such behavior. We assume we know what the other person means. The result is resentment on both sides. In the story, a student who is perhaps gifted is silenced. The repercussions of curtailing the learning of this student may go well beyond the classroom. Maybe this student would have become a great teacher himself but for this incident. Many future Einsteins may have been stopped in their learning because of this kind of event, never to realize their potential.

The purpose of this book is to examine such stories and ask such questions. It reflects the traditional Jewish way of reading, a methodology that is closer to studying and that involves careful consideration of each element in the text. It is my hope that this approach will help the reader to appreciate more fully the meaningful and artistic tales of our ancient tradition, as well as the challenging questions that arise from such study.

The Tales

Rabbi Chiyya and His Wife, the Prostitute

B. Talmud *Kiddushin* 81b

1 חִיָּא בַּר אַשִׁי הָיָה רָגִיל כָּל פַּעַם שֶׁהָיָה נוֹפֵל עַל פָּנָיו שֶׁהָיָה אוֹמֵר: הָרַחֲמָן יַצִּילֵנִי מִיֵּצֶר הָרַע.

2 יוֹם אֶחָד שְׁמָעַתּוּ אִשְׁתּוֹ.

3 אָמְרָה: הֲרֵי כַּמָּה שָׁנִים שֶׁפָּרוּשׁ מִמֶּנִּי – מָה טַעַם אוֹמֵר כָּךְ?

4 יוֹם אֶחָד הָיָה לוֹמֵד בְּגִנָּתוֹ.

5 קִשְּׁטָה עַצְמָהּ חָלְפָה וּבָאָה לְפָנָיו.

6 אָמַר לָהּ: מִי אַתְּ?

7 אָמְרָה לוֹ: אֲנִי חֲרוּתָא שַׁבְתִּי מֵהַיּוֹם.

8 תְּבָעָהּ.

9 אָמְרָה לוֹ: הָבֵא אֵלַי רִמּוֹן זֶה שֶׁבְּרֹאשׁ הָעָנָף.

10 קָפַץ וְהֵבִיאוֹ לָהּ.

11 כְּשֶׁבָּא לְבֵיתוֹ הָיְתָה אִשְׁתּוֹ מַסֶּקֶת אֶת הַתַּנּוּר.

12 עָלָה וְיָשַׁב בְּתוֹכוֹ.

13 אָמְרָה לוֹ: מַה זֶּה?

14 אָמַר לָהּ: כָּךְ וְכָךְ הָיָה מַעֲשֶׂה.

15 אָמְרָה לוֹ: אֲנִי הָיִיתִי.

16 אָמַר לָהּ: אֲנִי מִכָּל מָקוֹם לְאִסּוּר כִּוַּנְתִּי.

❦ 3 ❦

1. Whenever R. Chiyya bar Ashi would pray by himself it was his custom to say, "May the Merciful One save me from sexual transgression."

2. One day his wife heard him.

3. "Let us see," she reflected, "it is so many years that he has held aloof from me. Why then should he pray thus?"

4. One day, he was studying in his garden.

5. She adorned herself and repeatedly walked up and down before him.

6. "Who are you?" he demanded.

7. "I am Charuta, and have returned today," she replied.

8. He desired her.

9. She said to him, "Bring me that pomegranate from the uppermost bough."

10. He jumped up, went, and brought it to her.

11. When he reentered his house, his wife was firing the oven.

12. He ascended and sat in it.

13. "What's the meaning of this?" she demanded.

14. He told her what had befallen.

15. "It was I," she assured him.

16. "Nevertheless," said he, "my intention was evil."

When it comes to dysfunctional family relationships, we might think that the last few decades have seen far more sadness and disharmony than ever before. But as the story above points out, such dysfunction was not unknown to the rabbinic families of fifteen hundred years ago. True to the storytelling style of the Talmud, there are few details given in this brief tale, but the domestic picture is painted thoroughly enough for the reader to sense the unhappiness and confusion of this couple. Since the details in the story are sparse, the story must be read carefully. The following questions are provided in order to help the reader in this endeavor. Consider the questions while looking once again at the tale. The purpose of these questions is to slow down our minds so that we can better appreciate the nuances embedded in this miniature story.

Questions

1. "Whenever R. Chiyya bar Ashi would pray by himself it was his custom to say, 'May the Merciful One save me from sexual transgression.'" At this point in the story, what might be R. Chiyya's motivation for this prayer? What is the significance of the word "Whenever"? What is the meaning of "it was his custom"?

2. When his wife hears this prayer, in what possible ways might she choose to interpret it? How *does* she interpret it?

3. In the past, how might R. Chiyya's wife have interpreted the reason for her husband's remaining aloof from her?

4. At this point in the story, how might one characterize the relationship between R. Chiyya and his wife?

5. How does R. Chiyya's wife respond to her husband's revelation? What are the possible motivations for her dressing up in disguise (in other words, what does she want to discover)?

6. "One day, he was studying in his garden." What is significant about the phrase "one day"? Why does the event take place in R. Chiyya's garden?

7. At this point in the story, what are the possible reasons for his wife's adorning herself? Why does she walk repeatedly up and down before him?

8. "Who are you?" demands R. Chiyya. What is the significance of this question?

9. According to the famous medieval talmudic commentator Rashi, Charuta was the name of a well-known prostitute. In the Talmud, the word also means "wrinkled." What might be the meaning behind this word play?

10. How does R. Chiyya respond to "Charuta"? Is his response a surprise?

11. Why does she tell R. Chiyya to bring her a pomegranate?

12. "He jumped up, went, and brought it to her." What might be noteworthy about the form of this sentence?

13. What takes place between the time Chiyya brings her the fruit and when he reenters the house?"

14. "What's the meaning of this?" R. Chiyya's wife demands when he sits in the hot oven. What are R. Chiyya's possible motivations? What is ironic about his sitting in the burning oven?

15. "Nevertheless, my intention was evil." What does Chiyya mean by this declaration?

Obviously, many of the above questions can be answered in various ways. A miniature story such as this one contains a lot more meaning if it is read methodically. Since the two characters in the story, R. Chiyya and his wife, choose not to express their honest thoughts with each other, and since the narrator chooses not to tell us everything they are thinking, the reader must consider the different possible motivations for their behavior.

For instance, there is the image of R. Chiyya praying privately. This custom is not unusual for traditional Jews; but, in this case, is it really private? After all, his wife is able to overhear him. Was this an accident or a "passive aggressive" attempt on Chiyya's part to share this information with his wife? Read literally, R. Chiyya is asking for protection from the evil urge (yetzer hara). According to rabbinic thinking, the evil urge is responsible for our selfishness, possessiveness, and general ego needs. But as Freud would later point out, the evil urge is tied in inexorably with sexual urges. Therefore, when he says out loud that he needs protection from the evil urge, his wife clearly understands that he is afraid of sexual passion.

What seems to trouble her is the contrast between this plea and his putative lack of sexual interest in her. One can imagine his telling her a long time ago that he had no more interest in sex. And now she cannot understand what is going on. A more emotionally mature woman, we might argue, would confront her husband concerning this paradox, but this is not the case with the couple. Instead, she bides her time. When she sees him studying one day in the garden, she decides to act. The setting of the garden itself is not coincidental. It functions as a bridge between the home and the House of Study; like the Garden of Eden, it suggests sensual pleasures.

There are a number of explanations as to why R. Chiyya's wife dresses up as Charuta. She may well believe she will fool her husband and therefore is seeking to trick him. It is also possible that she doesn't plan to fool him and merely wishes to spice up their love life a little, especially if his interest in sex is more active than he has allowed her to believe. One can easily imagine this woman dressing up and walking repeatedly before her studious husband, desperately trying to get his attention. And one can imagine her disappointment when finally, looking up, he plaintively asks, "Who are you?" Is she disappointed that her disguise worked so well? Perhaps he knows who she is and is merely playing along?

When R. Chiyya's wife calls herself Charuta, it may be that she is, as Rashi suggests, pretending to be a prostitute. Or maybe she is simply playing a game, teasing her husband. And perhaps she is punning on the fact that although, like the meaning of the word, she is wrinkled and old, she still can be sexy if her husband is a willing partner. R. Chiyya certainly does seem willing, although it is not clear if he knows the real identity of the woman. Based on the later developments in the story, it seems most likely that he does in fact think she is a prostitute.

She demands that he do something for her, obtaining a pomegranate from a tree. The symbolism of the pomegranate is clear when we consider its appearance in the Song of Songs, the collection of biblical love (and at times erotic) poetry. It is also significant how this old man quickly jumps up and does whatever she desires. Even the structure of the sentence reflects R. Chiyya's suddenly sharp reflexes. Compare this to his practically ignoring the desires of his wife for so long. By giving her an object, the woman can later furnish it as proof that he was indeed with her. This motif is also found in the Bible, when Tamar, playing a prostitute, sleeps with her father-in-law, Judah, and later proves this by producing objects he had left with her (Genesis 38).

What happens between R. Chiyya's obtaining the fruit and the scene later in the kitchen is not provided but it does not take too much imagination to presume that his lust is consummated out in the garden. The author chooses not to give us these details, but instead focuses on the next scene, where the husband is visually depressed and ashamed for giving in to his sexual urges. He sits in the lit oven—an ironic place, given that his erotic passions have been burning and now his flesh will literally burn. Most readers expect that when he learns he has committed no sin, R. Chiyya will be relieved. His wife certainly can use the pomegranate to prove it was indeed she all along. But we learn that R. Chiyya is not appeased at all by this information. Indeed, it is irrelevant to him that he was with his wife and fulfilled her desires. His focus has been on controlling his desires, not meeting hers. From his perspective, sexuality is wrong. From her perspective, and possibly that of the narrator as well, ignoring one's wife is a far worse crime.

R. Chiyya mistakenly identifies evil as having sexual thoughts, even about one's wife. But the real sin is ignoring one's partner in life. Certainly Jewish thought developed a far more healthy view of sex than Rabbi Chiyya did. It would appear that he has been influenced more by Christianity or Platonic thought than by the more realistic approach toward human sexuality favored by the majority of his colleagues. For Chiyya, sex is bad, but ignoring his wife is not a sin. The basic moral of the story is that Chiyya indeed is sinning, but not in the way he thinks.

Pelimo and the Devil

B. Talmud *Kiddushin* 81b

1   פְּלֵימוֹ הָיָה רָגִיל שֶׁהָיָה אוֹמֵר: חֵץ בְּעֵינָיו הַשָּׂטָן.

2   יוֹם אֶחָד עֶרֶב יוֹם כִּפּוּר הָיָה.

3   נִדְמָה לוֹ (וְהַשָּׂטָן) כְּעָנִי. בָּא (וְ)קָרָא עַל הַפֶּתַח.

4   הוֹצִיאוּ לוֹ פַּת.

5   אָמַר לָהֶם: יוֹם כְּהַיּוֹם - כָּל הָעוֹלָם בִּפְנִים וַאֲנִי בַּחוּץ?

6   הִכְנִיסוּהוּ וְהֵבִיאוּ לְפָנָיו פַּת.

7   אָמַר: יוֹם כְּהַיּוֹם - כָּל הָעוֹלָם אֵצֶל הַשּׁוּלְחָן וַאֲנִי לְבַד?

8   הֵבִיאוּ וְהוֹשִׁיבוּהוּ אֵצֶל הַשּׁוּלְחָן.

9   הָיָה מַעֲלֶה עַל גּוּפוֹ שְׁחִין וַאֲבַעְבּוּעוֹת וְעוֹשֶׂה מַעֲשִׂים מְאוּסִים.

10   אָמְרוּ לוֹ: שֵׁב יָפֶה!

11   נָתְנוּ לוֹ כּוֹס - הִשְׁתָּעֵל בִּכְבֵדוּת וְיָרַק כִּיחוֹ לְתוֹכָהּ.

12   גָּעֲרוּ בוֹ.

13   נָפַל וָמֵת.

14   שָׁמַע (פְּלֵימוֹ) אוֹתָם שֶׁאוֹמְרִים: הָרַג פְּלֵימוֹ אָדָם...הָרַג פְּלֵימוֹ!

15   בָּרַח וְהִתְחַבֵּא בְּבֵית הַכִּיסֵּא.

16   הָלַךְ וְנָפַל לְפָנָיו.

17 כְּשֶׁרָאָה שֶׁהוּא מִצְטַעֵר גִּילָּה אֶת עַצְמוֹ בְּפָנָיו.

18 אָמַר לוֹ: מִפְּנֵי מָה אָמַרְתָּ כָּךְ?

19 אָמַר לוֹ: (וְאֶלָּא) אֵיךְ אוֹמַר?

20 אָמַר לוֹ: הָרַחֲמָן יִגְעַר בּוֹ בַּשָּׂטָן.

1 Pelimo used to say every day, "An arrow in Satan's eyes!"

2 One day—it was the eve of the Day of Atonement—

3 Satan disguised himself as a poor man and went and called out at his [Pelimo's] door.

4 Bread was brought out to him [Satan].

5 He pleaded, "On such a day when everyone is within, shall I be out?"

6 Thereupon he was taken in and bread was offered him.

7 "On a day like this," he urged, "when everyone sits at the table, shall I sit alone?"

8 He was led and sat down at the table.

9 As he sat, his body suddenly was covered with suppurating sores, and he behaved repulsively.

10 They told him, "Sit properly!"

11 They gave him a glass [of liquor] and he coughed and spat phlegm into it.

12 They scolded him.

13 He fell and died.

14 Then Pelimo heard people crying out: "Pelimo has killed a man! Pelimo has killed a man!"

15 He fled and hid in a bathroom.

16 Satan followed him and he fell before him.

17 When Satan saw how [Pelimo] was suffering, he disclosed his identity.

18 He asked Pelimo: "Why have you been cursing me?"

19 Pelimo asked, "Then how should I speak?"

20 [Satan] said to him, "[You should say] 'May the Merciful One rebuke Satan.'"

The tale of Pelimo fits into the genre of a horror story; Edgar Allan Poe might have written it. It is about a seemingly normal, average man undergoing a traumatic episode.

Questions

1. "Pelimo used to say every day, 'An arrow in Satan's eyes!'" What did Pelimo mean when he said these words? What does this statement teach us about Pelimo?

2. What is significant about the episode's occurring on the eve of the Day of Atonement (for the purposes of the story, we might translate it as "Day of Judgement")?

3. Why does Satan choose to appear as a poor man?

4. What is noteworthy about the following sentences?
   a. "Bread was brought out to him."
   b. "...he was taken in and bread was offered him."
   c. "He was led...."

5. What attitude characterizes Satan's response each time he receives something?

6. What is significant about the direction of Satan's movements?

7. How do the members of the household react to Satan's physical ailments? How else could they have responded?

8. What is significant about Satan's spitting into the glass?

9. Why does Satan choose to "die" at this time?

10. Why does Satan have people cry out: "Pelimo has killed a man! Pelimo has killed a man!"

11. Why does Pelimo flee to a bathroom?

12. Consider the phrase "he fell before him." Who falls before whom?
    a. Why might Satan fall before Pelimo?
    b. Why might Pelimo fall before Satan?
    c. What is significant about each interpretation?

13. "May the merciful One rebuke Satan." What is Satan trying to teach Pelimo?

14. Does Pelimo pass Satan's judgment? Why or why not?

Although a miniature story such as this one about Pelimo can be understood without considering its contextual placement in the Talmud, it is instructive to know that the tale comes amid other stories of righteous Sages. In each case the sage boasts that Satan (here representing the evil, or sexual, urge) has no power over him. Pelimo places himself in this category by his constant declaration that Satan (or the evil urge) has no power over him. A modern corollary might be the example of one-time presidential candidate Gary Hart, who told reporters they could follow him around because he had nothing to hide.

It turned out, however, that his morality was suspect; after photographers caught him gallivanting on a boat named *Monkey Business* Hart's presidential ambitions were ruined.

The rabbis taught that it was not wise to give Satan an excuse to bother one's self (Midrash *Vayikra Rabbah* 21:10). By boldly stating that he was above temptation, Pelimo was actually challenging Satan to try and tempt him. In other similar talmudic stories, the temptation usually comes in the form of a beautiful woman who successfully entices the moral paragon. In this case, Satan takes a more creative approach. He appears not as a sexual temptress but as a homeless person.

The evening on which Satan chooses to appear is the eve of Yom Kippur. Jews are preparing to fast and pray by eating a large meal. It is a time for spiritual preparation as well as material observance. As we see in many synagogues today, people dress up for Yom Kippur. Often they make it a formal and even somewhat extravagant event. Traditional Jews, on the other hand, play down such materialism by dressing simply in white and not wearing any leather. Even so, some traditional Jews devote so much attention to *not* dressing up, that it becomes a kind of materialism in its own way. In other words, the intentions of these Jews are not as spiritual as they may think, which may also be true in Pelimo's house.

The Pelimo household is sitting down to a fine dinner. They are enjoying the start of the spiritual day to come. When Satan appears in the guise of a homeless person, he is not part of the planned events, and so he upsets the normal order of the household. The people are focusing on

God's forthcoming judgment of them and are preparing to ask God for mercy. And right in front of them is a man in need of such mercy; a man who will be testing them, or more precisely, testing Pelimo. This will be his Day of Judgment in more ways than one.

Posing as a beggar, Satan keeps asking for attention. The household staff attempts, as many of us might, to give the homeless person as little attention as possible and to send him away. To each rebuff Satan complains that everyone is "within" while he is "without." He literally says that "all the world" is within. He is asking to be a part of the world. The household, however, takes his complaint literally. Instead of addressing the underlying needs of the "beggar" they simply usher him inside. In effect, they do whatever they can to appease him without helping him. What they really want is for him to go away. They do the least possible for him in the hopes of satisfying him enough so that he will leave. They see him not as a person, but as a problem to be solved.

It is also true that he is going to ruin their dinner party. After all, although it may be the eve of Yom Kippur, there is an aesthetic value to the day. The table is set with the best dishes. The manners are stately and formal. The diners are enjoying one another's company. Satan will ruin all of that. He will behave despicably. From the point of view of the household, he is a rude, ugly man. What they don't see is that in actuality he is a sick, desperate man in need of more attention than they are willing to provide. He is dying, and they are worried about the carpet.

After he apparently dies, Satan arranges it so that people think Pelimo has killed him. On the surface this seems odd. After all, it wasn't only Pelimo who was at the dinner, even if it is his house. Surely the blame should be shared. In addition, is it fair to say that the man was killed, or is it simply that his dying condition was not recognized until it was too late? Regardless, these considerations miss the point. It is only Pelimo who has been going around claiming to be so righteous that he cannot be tempted by Satan. Pelimo is holding himself up to a higher standard. And he has grievously failed to meet that standard. It might be permissible for someone to say he or she is not so good but not so evil either, and behave as Pelimo does. But if one claims to be righteous, one cannot be passively good. A righteous person must seriously attempt to help others. It's not enough to refrain from adultery. That's not righteousness: that's simply not being evil.

All of this is too much for Pelimo to handle. He clearly knows that he has gone from being a self-proclaimed righteous man to being a murder suspect—and this even before *Kol Nidrei* has been sung! By fleeing into the bathroom he has retreated to the center of the house, away from the cares and burdens of the outside world. (It is possible that the phrase *beit hakisei* refers not to the bathroom but to some place of shelter outside the city. Either way, the central theme is one of escape.) By fleeing, he also fails to observe another commandment, that of taking care of the dead.

When Satan appears before him it is not clear who falls down. It is understandable that Pelimo would fall, in surprise and fright. After all, he had thought the man was dead. Satan may also interpret this act as one of contrition on Pelimo's part. Pelimo has gone from being a moral paragon to falling down in the bathroom before a poor, homeless man thought to be dead.

It is also possible that it is Satan who falls in front of Pelimo, a ghost dying one more time. In this case, it is the final straw that breaks Pelimo. There is literally no place for him to hide from the cruel realities of the world. His self-righteousness will not protect him from the genuine suffering of others.

In any event, this traumatic encounter will humble Pelimo, teaching him that he has no reason to feel morally smug. Indeed, the role of Satan here is not so much to judge Pelimo as it is to teach him humility. It is hoped that, in the future, Pelimo will learn to judge himself and place his actions in their proper perspective. He is not a bad man, but neither is he without moral blemish. He, too, can do better. And if he needs to make a statement concerning the evil urge, let it be to the effect that God, the Merciful One, should rebuke Satan, for no human being has earned that right.

Rabbi Simeon and the Ugly Man

B. Talmud *Taanit* 20a-b

מַעֲשֶׂה בְּרַבִּי שִׁמְעוֹן בֶּן אֶלְעָזָר שֶׁבָּא מִמִּגְדַּל גְּדוֹר. מִבֵּית רַבּוֹ. וְהָיָה 1
רוֹכֵב עַל הַחֲמוֹר וּמְטַיֵּל עַל שְׂפַת הַיָּם. וְהָיָה שָׂמֵחַ שִׂמְחָה גְדוֹלָה
שֶׁלָּמַד תּוֹרָה הַרְבֵּה.

נִזְדַּמֵּן לוֹ אָדָם אֶחָד שֶׁהָיָה מְכוֹעָר בְּיוֹתֵר. 2

אָמַר לוֹ: שָׁלוֹם עָלֶיךָ רַבִּי. 3

לֹא הֶחֱזִיר לוֹ. 4

אָמַר לוֹ: רֵיקָא. כַּמָּה מְכוֹעָר אוֹתוֹ הָאִישׁ. שֶׁמָּא כָּל בְּנֵי עִירְךָ 5
מְכוֹעָרִין כְּמוֹתְךָ?

אָמַר לוֹ: לֵךְ אֱמוֹר לָאוּמָּן שֶׁעֲשָׂאַנִי "כַּמָּה מְכוֹעָר כְּלִי זֶה שֶׁעָשִׂיתָ!" 6

כֵּיוָן שֶׁיָּדַע בְּעַצְמוֹ שֶׁחָטָא יָרַד מִן הַחֲמוֹר וְנִשְׁתַּטַּח לְפָנָיו 7

וְאָמַר לוֹ: נַעֲנֵיתִי לָךְ. מְחוֹל לִי. 8

אָמַר לוֹ: אֵינִי מוֹחֵל לָךְ עַד שֶׁתֵּלֵךְ וְתֹאמַר לָאוּמָן שֶׁעֲשָׂאַנִי 9
"כַּמָּה מְכוֹעָר כְּלִי זֶה שֶׁעָשִׂיתָ!"

הָיָה מְטַיֵּל אַחֲרָיו עַד שֶׁהִגִּיעַ לְעִירוֹ. 10

יָצְאוּ אַנְשֵׁי עִירוֹ לִקְרָאתוֹ. 11

וְאָמְרוּ לוֹ: שָׁלוֹם עָלֶיךָ רַבִּי. 12

אָמַר לָהֶם: לְמִי אַתֶּם קוֹרְאִים רַבִּי? 13

אָמְרוּ לוֹ: לְזֶה שְׁמַטֵּיל אַחֲרֶיךָ. 14

אָמַר לָהֶם: אִם זֶה רַבִּי אַל יִרְבּוּ כְּמוֹתוֹ בְּיִשְׂרָאֵל. 15

אָמְרוּ לוֹ: חַס וְשָׁלוֹם! מֶה עָשָׂה לְךָ? 16

אָמַר לָהֶם: כָּךְ וְכָךְ עָשָׂה לִי. 17

אָמְרוּ לוֹ: אַף־עַל־פִּי־כֵן מְחוֹל לוֹ. 18

אָמַר לָהֶם: הֲרֵינִי מוֹחֵל לוֹ וּבִלְבַד שֶׁלֹּא יְהֵא רָגִיל לַעֲשׂוֹת כֵּן. 19

מִיָּד נִכְנַס רַבִּי שִׁמְעוֹן בֶּן אֶלְעָזָר לְבֵית הַמִּדְרָשׁ 20

וְדָרַשׁ: לְעוֹלָם יְהֵא אָדָם רַךְ כְּקָנֶה וְאַל יְהֵא קָשֶׁה כְּאֶרֶז. 21

1. Rabbi Simeon was coming from Migdal Gedor, from the house of his teacher, and he was riding leisurely *[metayel]* on his donkey by the riverside, feeling happy and elated because he had studied much Torah.

2. He happened to meet an exceedingly ugly man.

3. The man said to him: "Peace be upon you, Rabbi."

4. He, however, did not return his greeting.

5. Instead, he said to him: "You ignoramus! You are so ugly! Is it possible that all your fellow citizens are as ugly as you?"

6. He replied, "I do not know. Go and tell the craftsman who made me, 'How ugly is the vessel that you have made!'"

7. When R. Simeon realized that he had done wrong, he dismounted from the donkey and prostrated himself before the man.

8. He said to him, "I submit myself to you; forgive me."

9. He replied, "I will not forgive you until you go and tell the craftsman who made me, 'How ugly is the vessel that you have made!'"

10   He [R. Simeon] walked *[metayel]* behind him until he reached his city.

11   All the people of the town came out to greet him.

12   They said to him, "Peace be upon you, Rabbi."

13   The man asked them, "Whom are you calling 'Rabbi'?"

14   They responded, "The man who is walking behind you."

15   He said to them, "If this man is a rabbi, may there not be any more like him in Israel!"

16   They said to him: "God forbid you should say this! What has he done to you?"

17   He replied, "Such and such a thing has he done to me."

18   They said, "Even so, forgive him."

19   He said, "I will forgive him, but only the condition that he does not act this way in the future."

20   After this R. Simeon son of R. Eleazar entered the House of Study.

21   He taught: "One should always be gentle as the reed and never unyielding as the cedar."

If we are honest with ourselves, then we should admit that there is a little bit of Rabbi Simeon in every one of us. Have there not been times when we have been enjoying a peaceful, beautiful moment only to have it interrupted by someone or something that did not fit into our idea of the aesthetic experience? I have a beautiful drive to work every day, but if I find my car stuck behind some ugly truck, then I resent the truck's ruining my pleasant moment.

Of course the story of Rabbi Simeon and the ugly man is about far more than a good donkey ride ruined. Fundamental issues concerning personal and divine responsibility, sensitivity, and repentance are addressed in the story.

Questions

1. How is Rabbi Simeon feeling at the beginning of the story? Why? Might there be more than one reason? How does the narrative *show* how he is feeling?

2. Why does the man he meets call him "Rabbi"?

3. What might be the motivation for Rabbi Simeon's rude response? What generalization is he making?

4. What is the sin that Rabbi Simeon commits?

5. The man responds by invoking the Almighty. At this point in the story, what might be his reason for doing so?

6. How does Rabbi Simeon respond to the comment? What are his options?

7. If the story were to end at this point, what would its overall message be?

8. Instead of accepting the rabbi's apology, the man repeats—word for word—his request. What is the significance of this request? Why does the man repeat it? How has the meaning changed?

9. At this point, Rabbi Simeon follows the man. The same verb, *metayel,* which was used to describe his riding leisurely (at the beginning of the story), is now used when he follows the man. How is the meaning different here?

10. What is significant about Rabbi Simeon's following the man?

11. When the townspeople greet Rabbi Simeon, the man immediately asks, "Whom are you calling 'Rabbi'?" What is significant about the question and its timing?

12. What is noteworthy about the townspeople's response: "The man who is walking behind you"?

13. What is significant about the man's reply to the people concerning what Rabbi Simeon did? In other words, what *isn't* said?

14. How does Rabbi Simeon respond to the accusation? (What other replies are possible, and why does he choose this particular response?)

15. Why do the townspeople insist that Rabbi Simeon be forgiven? What is significant about the man's reply? Is his forgiveness sincere? Why or why not?

16. At the end of the story, Rabbi Simeon enters the House of Study. What is noteworthy about this act? What has changed since the last time he was in a House of Study?

17. The story concludes with Rabbi Simeon reciting Scripture: "One should always be gentle as the reed and never unyielding as the cedar." (Note: In the Bible, the reed is generally seen as negative and the cedar as positive.)
    a. According to the townspeople—who in all likelihood follow the rabbi into the House of Study—who is the reed and who is the cedar?
    b. According to Rabbi Simeon, who is the reed and who is the cedar?

18. What overall message does the story seek to communicate?

As mentioned before, it is easy to identify with Rabbi Simeon's spiritual high as he leisurely rides high atop his donkey. Not only has he studied much Torah at his master's house, he is also now enjoying the beauty of the physical world. His life is in harmony and he is at one with the world. The physical and the spiritual are equal. All is good; all is beautiful.

Into this perfect harmony there comes a distortion: an exceedingly ugly man. When this man speaks to Rabbi Simeon, breaking his trance, the rabbi cannot respond in a civil way. His honest thoughts find expression in a nasty comment. It is possible to read the Hebrew differently, in which case it is the rabbi who speaks first and greets the ugly man, who does not comment. This interpretation would make Rabbi Simeon appear slightly better, having first made a nice remark and then becoming mean in response to the ugly man's ignoring him, but this reading of the story is a stretch. What *is* clear is that Rabbi Simeon insults the ugly man, a man who may have indeed recognized the rabbi and wanted only to honor him.

Rabbi Simeon's comment cannot, of course, be justified. But it *can* be explained. The ugly man represents a fissure in Rabbi Simeon's perfect world. If physical and spiritual beauty are one, then lack of physical beauty must mean lack of spiritual beauty, too. When he calls the ugly man an ignoramus (literally, an empty person), he implies that the man's ugliness must reflect an inner ugliness as well. The surface deformity must also be matched by a deformity of soul. If the man is ugly, then he must be evil too, or at least lacking in Torah.

The ugly man's lack of Torah is itself challenged by a clever response that he makes to the rabbi. By pointing out that God is responsible for his physical ugliness, the man teaches the rabbi a lesson he had not learned from his master: when we insult a human being we insult God. Thus Rabbi Simeon is not only rude, he is treading on blasphemy. In other words, if the ugly man is literally empty, then the vessel he has been given is damaged, and the Creator of the vessel must be indicted. His question challenges the rabbi: Is that what you really meant to say?

Rabbi Simeon quickly recognizes he has sinned and shows his remorse. His body language and his words are a perfect example of a repentant man. He clearly understands the gravity of his crime and wishes to make amends. Were the story to end here, it would be a nice, if rather didactic, tale of a scholar who learned a good lesson. But the story does not end here. It continues, and by doing so it seeks to teach a very different lesson.

The ugly man chooses not to accept the apology. Instead he repeats verbatim his former request. The rabbi must have a conversation with God. The man is not making a rhetorical remark; rather, he wishes the rabbi to die and then speak with God. In effect, the conditions for accepting forgiveness are made impossible. At this point one could not blame Rabbi Simeon for going on his way, knowing that he tried to make amends. But instead he chooses to follow the ugly man, perhaps hoping for another chance. Ironically, the same word in Hebrew is used for his following the man as was used for Rabbi Simeon's leisurely ride. Although the word is the same, the experience could not be more different. Consider the word "tour," an English equivalent of *metayel*. It could refer to something pleasant, as in a sightseeing tour, or it could mean something difficult and dangerous, as in a military tour of duty.

When the townspeople greet the rabbi, they use language similar to that of the ugly man. This time, the rabbi makes no response. Perhaps in his humility he feels there is nothing for him to say. Instead, the ugly man chimes in, making sure the townspeople know the truth about this well-known teacher. Interestingly enough, he reports the story in such a way to make the rabbi look as bad as possible, with no mention of the rabbi's attempts to make amends.

The contrast between the meek behavior of the rabbi—following the ugly man for some distance, being led by him wherever he goes, keeping silent in the face of character attacks—and the accusations of the ugly man wins back for Rabbi Simeon the reader's favor. The townspeople, too, seem to know enough about the rabbi to appeal to the ugly man for forgiveness. Or, perhaps they are defending the sanctity of the rabbinic office. Maybe the obviously repentant behavior of the rabbi also convinces them to support him. The ugly man agrees to forgive the rabbi, at least publicly, but clearly there is little motivation on his part to be forgiving.

When the rabbi chooses to speak it is in the House of Study, and his words appear ambiguous. He declares: "One should always be gentle as the reed and never unyielding as the cedar." Upon hearing this, the townspeople probably think he is condemning himself. His black-and-white view of the world led him to insult a man for the "sin" of simply being ugly. The rabbi is the cedar and the ugly man who forgives him is the reed. Most likely this is the lesson the rabbi wants the people to believe. But between himself and God he views things differently. He is the reed, willing to learn from his mistakes and repent. The ugly man is the unyielding cedar, rigid in his inability to offer forgiveness. Which is the greater sin?

Furthermore, in biblical symbolism the cedar is a positive symbol in the Bible and the reed is a negative symbol. So how can a reed be called good and a cedar bad? Perhaps Rabbi Simeon is suggesting that generalizations can be deceiving. Just as he was wrong to think that an ugly man is a stupid man, and just as the townspeople will wrongly condemn the rabbi, so too one should be careful in condemning others. Not all cedars are good, and not all reeds are bad.

A careful reading of the tale shows that the structure of the story is designed in a particular way. Turn back to the story and notice the parallels and contrasts between the first half and the second half. In the first half, Rabbi Simeon is riding leisurely. In the second half he is following anxiously. In the first half the meeting is between the rabbi and the ugly man. In the second half the meeting is between the ugly man and the townspeople. In the first half the rabbi insults the ugly man. In the second half the ugly man insults the rabbi. In the first half the rabbi asks for forgiveness. In the second half the townspeople ask for forgiveness on the rabbi's behalf. In the first half the ugly man makes forgiveness impossible. In the second half forgiveness is made possible. Also, in the first half Rabbi Simeon has just left the House of Study. In the second half he enters the House of Study.

What do these comparisons suggest? Perhaps in some ways nothing has changed, and in some ways everything has changed. The second half of the story reflects the first half except for one vital difference: Rabbi Simeon has learned from his mistake. He is not the same man he was when riding leisurely away from his master's house. He has learned something about himself and has grown. He is not rigid like the cedar but flexible like the reed. And despite what the villagers may think, this is both a compliment and a genuine spiritual accomplishment.

The Laughter and the Angel of Death

Midrash *D'varim Rabbah* 9

1 מַעֲשֶׂה בְּרַבִּי שִׁמְעוֹן בֶּן חֲלַפְתָּא שֶׁהָלַךְ לִבְרִית מִילָה וְסָעַד שָׁם.

2 הִשְׁקָה אוֹתָם אָבִיו שֶׁל תִּינוֹק יַיִן יָשָׁן בֶּן שֶׁבַע שָׁנִים.

3 אָמַר לָהֶם: מִן הַיַּיִן הַזֶּה אֲנִי מְיַשֵּׁן לְשִׂמְחָתוֹ שֶׁל בְּנִי.

4 הָיוּ סוֹעֲדִים עַד חֲצִי הַלַּיְלָה.

5 רַבִּי שִׁמְעוֹן בֶּן חֲלַפְתָּא שֶׁהָיָה בָּטוּחַ עַל כּוֹחוֹ יָצָא בַּחֲצִי הַלַּיְלָה לֵילֵךְ לְעִירוֹ.

6 מָצָא שָׁם מַלְאַךְ הַמָּוֶת בַּדֶּרֶךְ וְרָאָה אוֹתוֹ מְשַׂחֵק.

7 אָמַר לוֹ: מִי אַתָּה?

8 אָמַר לוֹ: שְׁלוּחוֹ שֶׁל הַקָּבָּ"ה.

9 אָמַר לוֹ: וּמִפְּנֵי מָה אַתָּה מְשַׂחֵק?

10 אָמַר לוֹ: מִשִּׂיחָתָן שֶׁל בְּרִיּוֹת.

11 הֵן אוֹמְרוֹת "כָּךְ וְכָךְ אָנוּ עֲתִידִים לַעֲשׂוֹתִי" וְאֵינָן יוֹדְעוֹת אֵימָתַי הֵן נִקְרָאוֹת.

12 אוֹתוֹ הָאִישׁ הָיָה אוֹמֵר "מִן הַיַּיִן הַזֶּה אֲנִי מְיַשֵּׁן לְשִׂמְחָתוֹ שֶׁל בְּנִי" וַהֲרֵי הִגִּיעַ פִּרְקוֹ לִיטּוֹל אַחַר שְׁלוֹשִׁים יוֹם.

13 אָמַר לוֹ: הַרְאֵה לִי אֶת פִּרְקִי.

אָמַר לוֹ: לֹא עָלֶיךָ וְלֹא עַל כַּיּוֹצֵא בְּךָ אֲנִי שׁוֹלֵט. 14

פְּעָמִים שֶׁהַקְבָּ"ה חָפֵץ בְּמַעֲשֵׂיכֶם הַטּוֹבִים וּמוֹסִיף לָכֶם חַיִּים. 15

1   Simeon b. Chalafta went to a circumcision ceremony.

2   The father of the child made a feast and gave those present seven-year-old wine to drink.

3   He said to them: "Of this wine, I will store away a portion for my son's wedding feast."

4   The feast continued until midnight.

5   Rabbi Simeon, who trusted in his own strength, left at midnight to return to his city.

6   On the road the Angel of Death met him, and R. Simeon noticed he was laughing.

7   He [R. Simeon] asked him [the angel], "Who are you?"

8   The latter answered, "I am God's messenger."

9   He asked him, "Why are you laughing?"

10 He replied, "On the account of the talk of human beings.

11 They say, 'This and that we will do,' and yet not one of them knows when he will be summoned to die.

12 The man in whose feast you shared, and who said to you: 'Of this wine, I will store away a portion for my son's wedding feast,' lo, his [child's] time has come, he is to be snatched away after thirty days."

13 R. Simeon said to him, "Show me my end."

14 He replied, "Neither over you nor over the likes of you have I any dominion.

15 Often God finds delight in your good deeds and grants you additional life."

Like the story of Pelimo, the above tale has a ghoulish quality to it. Why did the ancient Sages create such stories? Perhaps they liked a good ghost story as much as we do today. However, there is also a serious message imbedded in this story about the Angel of Death, as we will see.

Questions

1. What is characteristic of the first "scene" of the story (that is, the circumcision feast)?

2. What is the significance of the mention of the son's wedding at his ritual circumcision?

3. What might be the meaning of Rabbi Simeon's trusting "in his own strength"? What might he have feared along the road?

4. At this point in the story, what might Rabbi Simeon think are the reasons for the Angel of Death's laughter? Why does R. Simeon ask the angel to identify himself?

5. What is significant about the angel's reply?

6. According to the angel, why is he laughing? What thinking (or feeling) is behind his laughter?

7. Consider the phrase "lo, his [child's] time has come." What is significant about the wording here?

8. What are the possible reasons for Rabbi Simeon's asking the angel about his own death?

9. What are the possible meanings of the angel's response: "Neither over you nor over the likes of you have I any dominion"?

10. What general view toward life and death is found in this story?

11. How might the story be divided into distinct parts? How do these parts differ in style?

The story begins at a *simchah,* a celebration. The second scene occurs on the road, late at night. Already there is a contrast between celebration and danger, between happiness and fear. Of course, when the story begins, the night and the road are not on the minds of the revelers. Rather, they are thinking about the new life before them. They are feasting and drinking special wine. There is light and jubilation. It is quite a different picture from that of the lone rabbi on the dark road.

The occasion of the celebration is the ritual circumcision, the *b'rit,* of the host's son. The host also mentions the son's future wedding. To mention the wedding at a *b'rit* is traditional, implying that one blessing will follow the other. These occasions are not only *simchahs,* joyous events; they are also mitzvot, divinely ordained life-cycle events. They imply an order and meaning in the universe. They are the tradition. And yet, ironically, the acts they celebrate, birth and love, are not themselves controllable. This is often the function of religious practice: creating order in a world that cannot be controlled.

In the second scene there are two basic issues to be resolved: the mortality of the baby and the mortality of Rabbi Simeon. Rabbi Simeon begins a journey that many people of his time would consider foolhardy. It was not wise to venture out at night. Trusting in his own strength probably does not mean that Rabbi Simeon felt he could defend himself from bandits or wild animals, but rather that his righteousness or Torah learning would invoke divine protection. He is counting on his adherence to the mitzvot to protect him from the unknown, from the uncontrollable.

When he confronts the Angel of Death, it is not clear whether or not Rabbi Simeon knows who the angel is. According to the story, the Angel of Death is laughing. Why does he laugh? Out there on the road, the effect may have been terrifying and not amusing, and yet the rabbi does not flee. Perhaps his curiosity gets the better of him.

When asked to identify himself, the Angel of Death describes himself as a messenger of God—a clerk, so to speak. He is not so much a terrifying apparition as he is an official functionary with a job to perform. He is not the enemy at all. He does not come to bestow punishment but simply to complete the will of his Creator. As he says to Rabbi Simeon, the child's "time has come." The infant's imminent death is not an accident, but rather part of a preordained, orderly plan. The Angel of Death is laughing because human beings apparently don't understand two important things about life: God has a plan, and humans don't know what it is. Not realizing these facts, people make their own plans and do not sufficiently realize how vulnerable such plans are to change. The angel laughs at humans' chutzpah, at their audacity. He laughs at a father who thinks that this son will live to be a groom instead of realizing that nothing is for certain.

Rabbi Simeon quickly changes the topic of conversation to himself. Given an opportunity to see the future, he cannot resist knowing his own end. It is perhaps surprising that he does not try to learn more information about the boy's imminent demise. Perhaps he could try to change the fate of the boy. (As we will see in the next story, such a thing is possible.) His interest in himself may bespeak a certain self-centeredness. It might also reflect an understandable anxiety. After all, why is the Angel of Death standing on the road with him? The angel's response reassures Rabbi Simeon that his business is not with him at that moment, but the words themselves are cryptic. What does the angel mean when he says he has no control over the likes of Rabbi Simeon? Is it because of the latter's high status? Or does he mean that adults can repent before it is too late, whereas babies cannot?

In general, the story implies that life and death are not direct results of reward and punishment, nor are they "good" and "bad" respectively. The baby does not deserve a short life. The Angel of Death is not an evil being. Life and death often just happen, with no reason that is apparent to us. It is true that righteousness may grant us longer life, but this is not a given. In the end, we should realize that we have no assurance of a tomorrow. All can be snatched away. Perhaps our celebrations should be tempered by this realization. And maybe this is why we break a glass at a wedding. In the midst of joy, even in the midst of doing a mitzvah, the ordered, predictable life we lead can disappear in a moment's time. Tragedy can come at any moment.

This tale is reminiscent of the famous story told by John O'Hara in his book *Appointment in Samarra*. In the story, a man believes that the Angel of Death is after him so he flees to Samarra. A friend of the man sees the Angel of Death and asks him where he is going. "To Samarra," he replies. "I have an appointment there." The lesson of this story, of course, is that we cannot cheat death. Our tale of Rabbi Simeon teaches us that we cannot take life for granted, but we can try to make an order out of the chaos. We can perform mitzvot. We can study. We can celebrate in the traditional ways. But we should never assume that such acts guarantee us long lives. For in life, all is given, but nothing is guaranteed.

Rabbi Akiva's Daughter

B. Talmud *Shabbat* 156b

1 רַבִּי עֲקִיבָה הָיְתָה לוֹ בַת.

2 אָמְרוּ לוֹ הָאִסְטְרוֹלוֹגִים: בַּיּוֹם שֶׁהִיא נִכְנֶסֶת לַחוּפָּה מַכִּישׁ אוֹתָהּ
   נָחָשׁ וְהִיא מֵתָה.

3 הָיָה דּוֹאֵג עַל הַדָּבָר הַרְבֵּה.

4 בַּיּוֹם שֶׁנִּכְנְסָה לַחוּפָּה נָטְלָה אֶת הַמַּכְבֵּנָה וְנָעֲצָה אוֹתָהּ בַּכּוֹתֶל.

5 קָרָה שֶׁנָּעֲצָה בְּעֵינוֹ שֶׁל נָחָשׁ.

6 בַּבּוֹקֶר כְּשֶׁנְּטָלָהּ אוֹתָהּ נִסְרַךְ נָחָשׁ אַחֲרֶיהָ.

7 אָמַר לָהּ אָבִיהָ: מֶה עָשִׂית?

8 אָמְרָה לוֹ: בָּעֶרֶב בָּא עָנִי וְקָרָא בַּפֶּתַח. הָיוּ כּוּלָּם טְרוּדִים בַּסְּעוּדָה
   וְלֹא שְׁמָעוּ.

9 קַמְתִּי אֲנִי. נָטַלְתִּי אֶת הַמָּנָה שֶׁנָּתַתָּ לִי וּנְתַתִּיהָ לוֹ.

10 אָמַר לָהּ: מִצְוָה עָשִׂית.

11 יָצָא וְדָרַשׁ: "צְדָקָה תַּצִּיל מִמָּוֶת" – לֹא מִיתָה מְשֻׁנָּה אֶלָּא
   מִמִּיתָה עַצְמָהּ.

1 Rabbi Akiva had a daughter.

2 Astrologers told him, "On the day she is to enter the bridal chamber, a snake will bite her and she will die."

3 He was very worried about this prediction.

4 On the day [of her marriage], she happened to be holding a long ornamental pin, which she stuck into the opening of a wall.

5 By chance, the pin penetrated the eye of the snake [coiled behind the wall] and remained stuck there.

6 The next morning, when she took out the pin, the dead snake was pulled out with it.

7 Her father asked, "Did you do anything unusual?"

8 She replied, "Last evening a poor man came to the door. Everybody was busy with the banquet, and no one heard him.

9 So I took the gift you had given me and gave it to the poor man."

10 "You have acted in a meritorious manner," he said to her.

11 And then R. Akiva went out and lectured: "'Charity delivereth from death' (Proverbs 10:2)—not [merely] from an unnatural death, but from death, whatever the cause."

This story is presented as a series of three scenes followed by a teaching of Rabbi Akiva. True to the style of a miniature tale, even the balanced division of the scenes reflects its careful composition. In the story, there is a warning about an event, then the event itself, and finally a reflection about what happened. Based on what is said—and not said—we can learn something important about human nature and divine guidance.

Questions

1. What is the role of astrologers in determining people's future? To what might they be compared today?

2. Upon hearing their words, how might Akiva respond? How does he choose to respond?

3. What might Akiva mean when he asks his daughter, "Did you do anything unusual?" How does his daughter understand his question?

4. The characters in the story (the astrologers, Akiva, his daughter) act in ways that reflect their basic understandings of worldly cause and effect. What are these understandings, and how do they differ from one another?

5. This story is similar in many ways to that of Pelimo and Satan. What is the fundamental difference?

6. How do Akiva's three appearances in the story reflect his change of perspective concerning human influence on fate?

Although exterior knowledge of the life and teachings of the characters in our stories is not necessary to appreciate the teachings of the stories, it is useful here to know that Rabbi Akiva once made the following paradoxical statement: "All is foreseen and free will is given." Zen masters would call this a *koan*—or a nonsense statement that, upon reflection, contains great truth. How can all be foreseen (by God) if at the same time humans have free choice? It is this very question that our story seeks to address.

Astrologers in Akiva's time functioned as the financial analysts of their day. Their job was to consider the factors and make a prediction for the future. They did not attempt to change fate; rather, they simply "crunched the numbers" and announced the results. Astrologers became the experts because they could read the stars and tell people's fate. Today, when we offer someone congratulations in a Jewish context, we say "mazal tov." This phrase literally translates as "a good star"; figuratively, it means "may you have a good fate from a good star." When the astrologers tell Akiva the bad news about his daughter, they are in effect saying, "The earnings report came back and the outlook is not good." They are also like lab technicians offering a biopsy report, but instead of pathology they use astrology.

Upon hearing this bad news, Akiva has a number of choices. He can (1) make sure she never has a wedding, (2) decide not to take the prediction of the astrologers seriously, (3) or do nothing but still worry about it. Now, we might think that Akiva—as a believing Jew—would simply reject the astrologers' prediction. But in those days ignoring the astrologers would be like our not listening to financial analysts. So, even though Akiva would not worship the stars, he would take astrologers' predictions seriously. However, he apparently does not take them so seriously as to prevent his daughter from marrying. Thus, he finds himself taking the third choice: doing nothing but worrying anyway. This choice reflects Akiva's ambivalence about the "scientific" advice of the astrologers. He will not greatly alter his daughter's life because of it, but neither will he forget what they said. (Maybe we have heard a doctor tell us: "This irregularity is probably nothing. Don't worry about it." We may agree it's probably nothing but most of us will still worry about it.)

Does Akiva at least tell his daughter of the prediction? It seems not, since we read of no fear on her part. Perhaps he wanted to save her the anxiety, or perhaps he felt there was no need since he had no preventive advice to offer.

The middle scene of the story is presented in a matter-of-fact way. With apparent good luck, instead of the snake's killing her, she winds up killing the snake. There seems to be nothing going on except good fortune for the daughter. But as the third scene begins, Akiva, obviously relieved to see his daughter alive, asks her an interesting question: "Did you do anything unusual?"

At this point in the story Akiva may be asking a question regarding her physical behavior in the room. Does she always stick her jewelry there? Did she notice the snake before? But the question can also be interpreted from the point of view of righteousness. In other words, did she do something very righteous that might have affected a change in her fate? Akiva's daughter seems to understand the question this way and answers that, yes, she performed a mitzvah. It is also possible she doesn't understand the connection but still considers her helping a poor man unusual for her or her household, especially on her wedding night.

Compare the actions of Akiva's daughter and the rest of her household, to the behavior of Pelimo's household on Yom Kippur eve. At Pelimo's house, no one cares for the poor person, least of all Pelimo. Here, the bride of the wedding is the exception. As at Pelimo's house, the "world" (the literal Hebrew word) is too concerned with spiritual or social behavior to help a poor person. Only Akiva's daughter notices. And this sensitivity spares her life.

On the High Holy Days it is traditional for Jews to declare that *tzedakah,* prayer, and repentance can change our fate. Curiously enough, Akiva did not think of telling his daughter to engage in these in order to change her fate, but her own natural sensitivity helped her nonetheless.

It is instructive to compare the world views of the three characters in the story. The astrologers as a group read the stars and say what will happen. They believe in what we today call determinism. Fate has decreed your destiny; end of story. Akiva genuinely wants to believe in free will. He hopes that his daughter can escape her fate by her actions, although what actions we should take in order to escape our fate are not clear. The daughter acts with righteousness for no apparent reason. In other words, Akiva does not warn his daughter of her fate and instruct her to engage in prayer, repentance, and *tzedakah.* She appears to do so out of simple inherent goodness.

Akiva appears in the story three times, and each time he changes his perspective on the role human beings play in determining their fate. In the beginning, he believes enough in the prediction of the astrologers to be worried. Later, Akiva's question to his daughter belies his balancing his belief in the astrologers with the possibility that human goodness can affect fate. And, in the end, he teaches that, indeed, how we behave can change our fate. Akiva's teaching at the end does not exactly fit the context of the story. *Tzedakah* (charity) can save from death, even unnatural death, but only for a time. Regardless of one's actions eventually death is inevitable. Nevertheless, the moral seems clear. All is foreseen (there is fate); but we can change fate by our noble actions (free will).

In comparing this story with that of Pelimo and Satan, one more difference stands out. In Pelimo's story, Pelimo liked to say "an arrow in Satan's eyes," but in the end it is Pelimo who is vanquished. In the story of Akiva's daughter, she literally puts the pin in the eye of the serpent (often associated with Satan). It is as if we all are being told: Worry not about what you say but about what you do. And what you should do is practice righteousness. It may not save you from a tragic death, but then again it might. Certainly it will make you worthy of being saved, and along the way you will help a lot of needy people.

Joseph the Sabbath Lover

B. Talmud *Shabbat* 119a

יוֹסֵף מוֹקִיר שַׁבָּתוֹת – הָיָה גּוֹי בִּשְׁכוּנָתוֹ שֶׁהָיוּ נְכָסָיו מְרֻבִּים. 1

אָמְרוּ לוֹ הַכַּלְדִּיִּים: כָּל הַנְּכָסִים יוֹסֵף מוֹקִיר שַׁבָּתוֹת אוֹכֵל אוֹתָם. 2

הָלַךְ וּמָכַר אֶת כָּל הַנְּכָסִים. 3

קָנָה בָּהֶם מַרְגָּלִית וְקָבַע אוֹתָהּ בְּסָדִינוֹ. 4

כַּאֲשֶׁר עָבַר בַּמַּעְבּוֹרוֹת הַפְּרִיחָה הָרוּחַ אֶת סְדִינוֹ 5

וְהֵטִילָה אוֹתוֹ בַּמַּיִם וּבָלַע אוֹתוֹ דָג. 6

הוֹצִיאוּהוּ וֶהֱבִיאוּהוּ לִפְנוֹת עֶרֶב שַׁבָּת. 7

אָמְרוּ: מִי קוֹנֶה בְּשָׁעָה זֹאת? 8

אָמְרוּ לָהֶם: לְכוּ וֶהֱבִיאוּהוּ לְיוֹסֵף מוֹקִיר שַׁבָּתוֹת שֶׁרָגִיל לִקְנוֹת. 9

הֱבִיאוּהוּ אֶצְלוֹ וְקָנָה אוֹתוֹ. 10

קָרַע אוֹתוֹ וּמָצָא בּוֹ מַרְגָּלִית. 11

מָכַר אוֹתָהּ בִּשְׁלוֹשׁ־עֶשְׂרֵה עֲלִיּוֹת שֶׁל דִּינָרֵי זָהָב. 12

פָּגַשׁ בּוֹ זָקֵן אֶחָד. אָמַר 13

מִי שֶׁמַּלְוֶה לַשַּׁבָּת הַשַּׁבָּת פּוֹרַעַת לוֹ. 14

1   Joseph-who-honors-the-Sabbath had in his neighborhood a certain gentile who owned a lot of property.

2   Soothsayers told him: All the property you have, Joseph-who-honors-the-Sabbath will eventually enjoy.

3   So the gentile went and sold his property.

4   With the proceeds he bought a pearl, which he secured in his headdress.

5   When he was crossing a bridge the wind blew off the headdress.

6   It carried it out to sea, and a fish swallowed it.

7   The fish was caught and brought to the marketplace on the eve of the Sabbath at twilight.

8   They asked, "Who will buy a fish at this late hour?"

9   They were told, "Go, take it to Joseph-who-honors-the-Sabbath. He is always eager to buy [fine food in the Sabbath's honor].

10   So the fish was brought to him and he bought it.

11   When he cut it open he found the pearl in it.

12   He sold it for enough gold denars to fill thirteen upper chambers.

13   A certain venerable elder met him and said:

14   "He who lends to the Sabbath, the Sabbath will repay him."

Just as in the last story, here, too, a prediction of the future plays an important role. Once again, a prediction is made and once again the question of its coming true is at the center of the story. In this case, the story is about a man known as "Joseph-who-honors-the-Sabbath." Why he is called this name will become clear later in the story.

Questions

1. The jewel in the story is transferred from the gentile to Joseph by means of the wind, the water, and the fish. What do these three things have in common?

2. What else is responsible for the jewel's coming into Joseph's possession? What is different about this means?

3. Joseph and Rabbi Akiva's daughter (see the previous story) both act out of a similar motivation. How would one characterize this motivation?

4. What exactly is the lesson that the old man shares with Joseph?

5. How does the old man's view of fate differ from that of the soothsayers?

The story begins with a description of Joseph as a ritually oriented Jew, but the significance of this orientation is not explained. Then the rich man, Joseph's neighbor, learns that he must act in order to prevent Joseph's receiving his possessions. The man obviously takes the prediction of the soothsayers seriously; nonetheless, he believes he can outwit fate. But the supernatural actions of the wind, water, and fish ensure that such an attempt will fail: God wants Joseph to have the wealth.

However, more than supernatural means are needed for Joseph to receive the jewel. He himself also plays a part. After all, if he were not so devoted to the Sabbath, then the people in the market would not think of selling the fish to him. Indeed, at this late hour before the Sabbath, the fish might have been thrown away were it not for Joseph's reputation. It is ironic that Joseph, like Akiva's daughter, has no knowledge of the play in which he acts. Like Akiva's daughter, he is simply doing the right thing. In her case her righteousness is manifested through ethics; in Joseph's case it is through ritual observance. For Judaism, the two are equal.

Upon meeting Joseph, the old man teaches him that one who honors the Sabbath will be repaid. In other words, one who lends his time and money into making the Sabbath holy will receive a good return on his investment. Although this is usually taken in a spiritual context, the storyteller wants us to believe that we will also benefit financially from resting on and honoring the Sabbath.

But the lesson is greater than a call for Sabbath observance. Implicit in the story is a recognition that how we act determines our fate. It's not that we should try to control our destiny. Look what happened when the gentile attempted this feat. The very thing he feared occurred. What we *should* do is live our lives in such a way that we are hopeful for a good outcome, even though there is no such guarantee. We should "do the right thing" for the sake of doing the right thing and let the consequences take care of themselves.

In one respect Rabbi Akiva's daughter and Joseph are complete opposites: the daughter's good actions change her fate, while Joseph's good behavior ensures that fate occurs as predicted. But this difference is superficial. The same cause and effect is at work. As Akiva declared: "All is foreseen [by God] and free will is given." Yes, God knows what will happen in the end, but individuals cannot know. What we *can* do is try to make the right choices, ritually as well as ethically.

The Late Return

B. Talmud *K'tubot* 62b

1 רַבִּי חֲמָא בַּר בִּיסָא הָלַךְ וְיָשַׁב שְׁתֵּים־עֶשְׂרֵה שָׁנִים בְּבֵית רַבּוֹ.

2 כְּשֶׁחָזַר אָמַר: לֹא אֶעֱשֶׂה כְּמוֹ בֶּן חֲכִינַאי.

3 נִכְנַס יָשַׁב בְּבֵית הַמִּדְרָשׁ וְשָׁלַח לְבֵיתוֹ.

4 בָּא רַבִּי אוֹשַׁעְיָא בְּנוֹ וְיָשַׁב לְפָנָיו.

5 הָיָה שָׁאַל אוֹתוֹ בַּהֲלָכָה.

6 רָאָה שֶׁתַּלְמִידוֹ חָרִיף.

7 חָלְשָׁה דַעְתּוֹ.

8 אָמַר: אִילוּ הָיִיתִי כָּאן הָיָה לִי בֵּן כָּזֶה.

9 נִכְנַס (רַבִּי חֲמָא) לְבֵיתוֹ.

10 נִכְנַס (בְּנוֹ) אַחֲרָיו.

11 עָמַד (רַבִּי חֲמָא) לְפָנָיו. סָבַר לִשְׁאֵלוֹ בַּהֲלָכָה הוּא רוֹצָה.

12 אָמְרָה לוֹ אִשְׁתּוֹ: הַאִם יֵשׁ אָדָם שֶׁקָּם מִלְּפְנֵי תִנוֹקוֹ?

1   Rabbi Chama bar Bar Bisa went away [from home] and spent twelve years at the House of Study.

2   When he returned he said, "I will not act as did Ben Chachinai."

3   He therefore entered the [local] House of Study and sent word to his house.

4   Meanwhile his son, Rabbi Oshaia, entered and sat down before him.

5   R. Oshaia addressed to him a question concerning the Law.

6   He saw how well versed he was in his studies.

7   He became very depressed.

8   He said to himself, "Had I been here, I also could have had such a child."

9   He entered his house.

10   His son came after him.

11   R. Chama rose before him, thinking that he wished to ask him some further legal questions.

12   His wife said to him: "What kind of man stands up before his son?"

Obviously this story can only be properly understood when we know about the actions of Ben Chachinai; fortunately, the tale is recounted in a midrashic commentary to Genesis that will be provided later in the chapter. Even without the story of Ben Chachinai, however, we can learn a great deal from the homecoming of Rabbi Chama.

Questions

1. Why does Rabbi Chama leave home for twelve years to study abroad? At this point in the story, what might have motivated his absence? Why does Rabbi Chama choose to return now?

2. What might Ben Chachinai have done? What do we learn about Rabbi Chama's character from this declaration?

3. Why does Rabbi Chama choose to enter the local study house and send word from there?

4. What characterizes the meeting between father and son? Is the meeting coincidental?

5. What are the possible reasons, based on what we know at this point in the story, for Rabbi Chama's becoming depressed?

6. "Had I been here, I also could have had such a child." What is Rabbi Chama thinking at this time and why?

7. What characterizes the meeting between husband and wife?

8. Why might Rabbi Chama mistake his son's intention?

9. What is the significance of his wife's question, "What kind of man stands up before his son?"

10. After reading the story of Ben Chachinai (below) compare his behavior with that of Rabbi Chama. In what ways are the two men's actions alike? In what ways are they different?

The tale before us is not as unusual for its time as we might think. Seventeen hundred years ago, scholars often spent a great deal of time away from home in order to receive the best education they could find. Whether they were simply seeking a better education or were also conveniently releasing themselves from family duties and distractions is of course an appropriate question. It is hard to know their genuine motivations. But we do know that there was a great deal of scholarly travel between Palestine and Babylon, and with it long absences from family.

The story of Ben Chachinai provides another example:

> R. Chanina b. Chachinai and R. Simeon b. Yochai went to study Torah at R. Akiba's college at Bene Berak, and stayed there thirteen years. R. Simeon b. Yochai used to send home [for news] and knew what was happening at his house. R. Chanina did not send and did not know what was happening at his house.
>
> His wife sent him word and told him: "Your daughter is marriageable, come and get her married." [He said nothing to his master.] Nevertheless, R. Akiva saw it by means of the Holy Spirit and he said to him: "If anyone has a marriageable daughter he may go and get her married."
>
> R. Chanina understood what he meant, so he rose, took leave, and went. He sought to enter into

his house, but found its appearance had been changed [and so did not recognize it].

What did he do? He went and sat down at the place where the women draw water and heard the voices of the little girls saying: "Daughter of Chanina, fill your vessel and go."

What did he do? He followed her until she entered his house. He went in after her suddenly. No sooner did his wife see him then her soul departed.

Said he to God: "Sovereign of the Universe! Is that the reward of this poor woman, after thirteen years of waiting?" Thereupon her soul returned to her body. (Midrash *B'reishit Rabbah* 95)

This story fortunately has a happy ending, but obviously there are odd things going on in this family. The strangest element is that this scholar would spend thirteen years away in study and not continue to have an interest in his family. Clearly this cannot be seen as an ideal in Judaism. Ben Chachinai is no paragon of Jewish family values.

In our story it is clear that Rabbi Chama wants to be nothing like Ben Chachinai. He takes great pains to avoid the kind of surprise that could steal the soul of (that is, kill) his wife. Nevertheless, his general situation is similar. In both cases male scholars have decided to spend their lives away from their families. However, in our story of Rabbi Chama we only learn in line 4 that he has a son and in line 12 that he has a wife. In other words, our perception of him changes as the story unfolds. Not knowing exactly who Ben Chachinai was, we do not know that Rabbi Chama has a wife and fears scaring her to death. We only know that he has left his family. Of course this could refer to his parents and siblings. When we learn that he has left behind at least a wife and a son, his absence becomes far more troublesome. We also do not know that he has not kept in contact with his family (as Ben Chachinai also chose not to do) until later in the story, when it becomes clear he knows nothing of his son's intellectual prowess.

Now, Rabbi Chama does not need his teacher to tell him to return. Presumably he returns because of a desire to see his family. And presumably he wishes to be different than Ben Chachinai. When Rabbi Chama returns, he goes not to the place of gossip—that is, the well—but rather to the House of Study. Why does he go there? Perhaps he thinks he will find out about his family there. Or perhaps he wants to continue learning. After all, in his culture, to waste a minute when you could be learning is anathema. Perhaps he goes for purely practical and spiritual reasons to the House of Study.

When his son enters, the reader immediately knows who he is because of the narrator's intervention. Some readers may recognize the name of the son, who later becomes a famous teacher as well. But we need not think that either father or son knows who the other is at this point in the story. As it will turn out, the father certainly has no clue that the brilliant boy is his own son.

At first, it is not clear why Rabbi Chama becomes depressed. Is he upset because this boy is smarter than he is? Does he realize that he could have stayed at home and learned just as much—if not more—than what he learned while away for twelve years? As we can later surmise, his depression reflects the realization that his absence robbed him of the opportunity to teach his own son the lessons of Torah. It is ironic of course that his own son is an expert in Torah, but the tragic loss of relationship is still as brutal.

When Rabbi Chama goes home we learn nothing of the meeting with his wife. Obviously she does not die from shock or that would have been reported, and in a superficial way this means that Rabbi Chama has succeeded in his mission. His return has not killed his wife. Indeed, his return doesn't seem to make much difference at all. When his son comes in the house, Rabbi Chama still doesn't understand that he is the father of a great scholar. He assumes the boy has followed him home in order to challenge him. But Rabbi Chama has no interest in being challenged. His standing up effectively says there is nothing for me to teach you, so please do not come to me. It is a sign of respect but also resignation.

His wife's response is one of alarm. Why would her husband—a great scholar who has sacrificed twelve years away from his family for Torah—defer the authority of Torah learning to his son? In Hebrew the literal word is *tinok,* "baby." She still thinks of her boy as a child. How can Rabbi Chama tell her the truth, that by staying home their son has learned more than he himself has learned by going away? Perhaps he will not tell her. But Rabbi Chama knows that he has made a great mistake. In the end, he is exactly like Ben Chachinai. His homecoming may reflect more sensitivity, but the twelve years away speak for themselves.

The Eve of Yom Kippur

B. Talmud *K'tubot* 62b

1   רַב רְחוּמִי הָיָה מָצוּי לִפְנֵי רָבָא בְּמָחוֹזָא וְהָיָה רָגִיל שֶׁהָיָה בָּא לְבֵיתוֹ כֹּל עֶרֶב יוֹם הַכִּפּוּרִים.

2   יוֹם אֶחָד מָשְׁכָה אוֹתוֹ הַהֲלָכָה.

3   הָיְתָה מְצַפָּה אִשְׁתּוֹ:

4   עַכְשָׁיו בָּא. עַכְשָׁיו בָּא.

5   לֹא בָּא.

6   חָלְשָׁה דַּעְתָּהּ.

7   נָפְלָה דִּמְעָה מֵעֵינָהּ.

8   הָיָה יוֹשֵׁב בַּגַּג.

9   נָפַל הַגַּג מִתַּחְתָּיו וָמֵת.

1   R. Rechumi, who was frequenting [the school] of Rava at Machuza, used to return home on the eve of every Day of Atonement.

2   On one occasion he was so attracted by his subject [that he forgot to return home].

3   His wife was expecting [him every moment].

4   [She would say:] "He is coming soon. He is coming soon."

5   But he did not come.

6   She became depressed.

7   Tears began to flow from her eyes.

8   [At that moment] he was sitting on a roof.

9   The roof collapsed under him and he was killed.

The above story immediately reminds us of the sad tales of Rabbis Chama and Ben Chachinai albeit with some differences. Here, the drama happens on a very significant day—the same time frame as in Pelimo's story. This story is also truly a miniature tale. Very little seems to happen except that a scholar doesn't keep his word, his wife becomes depressed, and the scholar dies. Once again, however, a careful review of the story may afford us more insight into its meaning and relevance.

Questions

1. "R. Rechumi, who was frequenting [the school] of Rava at Machuza, used to return home on the eve of every Day of Atonement." What is surprising about this verse? What might the word "frequenting" imply? What is significant about it being the eve of Yom Kippur? What is implied by the word "every"?

2. "On one occasion he was so attracted by his subject [that he forgot to return home]." To which occasion does the story refer? What is surprising about R. Rechumi's actions?

3. "She became depressed." What is significant about the timing of her feelings?

4. "[At that moment] he was sitting on a roof. The roof collapsed under him and he was killed." What is significant about both what R. Rechumi is doing and where he is doing it? What is the meaning of the roof's collapse? Why does it collapse?

With such a short story it is obvious that symbolism must play a major role. The events described cannot simply be a "journalistic account" of what happened. They are rendered in a sparse way, but with enough information to teach a lesson. Especially given the absence of details, the symbolism itself helps convey the message. For instance, there is the name of the sage, Rechumi. The Hebrew means either "merciful" or "loving." This is an ironic title for a man who ignores his wife. He is anything but her lover, yet clearly he is a lover of Torah. Herein lies the dilemma. On the one hand, his faithfulness to Torah is commendable. On the other hand, ignoring his wife is inexcusable.

As the story unfolds, his abandonment of his wife becomes clear. At first we are told that he "frequents" the academy of Rava. The term might easily connote a casual relationship with the place. However, R. Rechumi's commit-ment to this fine academy and its well-known teacher is anything but informal. He *lives* there. He only returns home once a year, on the evening of Yom Kippur. In talmudic times, Yom Kippur eve served the same function that the first night of Passover serves in our day. It was the family night par excellence. And so his choosing to return home that day was recognition that at least once a year he had a duty to his wife. And apparently his wife was ready to accept this arrangement.

Returning home once a year proves too difficult for this scholar, however; one Yom Kippur eve his studies take his attention and he forgets to go or even to send word that he is not coming. The irony here is almost tragic: this devoted student of a great teacher, studying at a great academy, can't even manage to return home once a year to see his wife and presumably his larger family. As we have seen in other stories, Torah knowledge alone doesn't make one a decent human being.

The worst part is the timing. It is already Yom Kippur—too late for an opportunity for forgiveness to arrive. There will be no way to undo the damage. The scene back home is pathetic. The Torah-widow (already she is a widow for all intents and purposes) waits for her husband's return: "He is coming soon. He is coming soon." And then the sad realization dawns on her that he is not coming. A tear falls, foreshadowing the falling of the roof.

The collapse of a roof was probably not uncommon during this period. Buildings inherently were not safe. Some would say that the roof collapsed, and the presumption of Rechumi's guilt then follows. Others would like to believe that somehow God is punishing this would-be scholar. From a literary point of view, there is poetry in the roof's falling just as Rechumi's wife's tear falls. But the symbolism also reflects the basic lesson of the story: you can ignore your family and study on the roof, as close to God as possible, on the holiest night of the year. But this is not what God wants from us, even from the pious. God wants us to remember our families. We are to live in the real world and not only in the rarefied sphere of the academy. For the Torah was not given to be studied in a vacuum. Rather, the Torah is for people with family responsibilities and human sensitivities. It is for lovers of people, not merely for lovers of books.

The great twentieth-century scholar and social activist Abraham Joshua Heschel once reflected that when he was a young man he admired smart people. As he grew older he came to admire kind people more. The author of our tale does not give us this lesson in a straightforward way, but beneath the symbols and behind the terse drama lies the same basic message.

The Escape

Midrash *B'reishit Rabbah* 41

1   אֶחָיו שֶׁל רַבִּי אֱלִיעֶזֶר הָיוּ חוֹרְשִׁים בַּמִּישׁוֹר וְהוּא חוֹרֵשׁ בָּהָר.

2   נָפְלָה פָרָתוֹ וְנִשְׁבְּרָה.

3   אָמַר: לְטוֹבָתִי נִשְׁבְּרָה פָרָתִי.

4   בָּרַח.

5   הָלַךְ לוֹ אֵצֶל רַבָּן יוֹחָנָן בֶּן זַכַּאי.

6   הָיָה אוֹכֵל קוֹזְזוֹת אֲדָמָה עַד שֶׁעָשָׂה פִיו רֵיחַ רַע.

7   הָלְכוּ וְאָמְרוּ לְרִבִּ"ז: רֵיחַ פִיו שֶׁל אֱלִיעֶזֶר קָשָׁה.

8   אָמַר לָהֶם: כְּשֵׁם שֶׁהִבְאִישׁ רֵיחַ פִיו עַל הַתּוֹרָה כָּךְ יִהְיֶה רֵיחוֹ
      הוֹלֵךְ מִסוֹף הָעוֹלָם וְעַד סוֹפוֹ.

9   לְאַחַר יָמִים עָלָה אָבִיו לְנַדוֹתוֹ מִנְּכָסָיו.

10   מְצָאוֹ יוֹשֵׁב וְדוֹרֵשׁ וּגְדוֹלֵי הַמְּדִינָה יוֹשְׁבִים לְפָנָיו: בֶּן צִיצִית הַכֶּסֶף,
      נַקְדִּימוֹן בֶּן גּוּרְיוֹן, וּבֶן כַּלְבָּא שָׂבוּעַ.

11   אָמַר לוֹ אָבִיו: בְּנִי לֹא עָלִיתִי לְכָאן אֶלָּא לְנַדוֹתְךָ מִנְּכָסָי.
      עַכְשָׁיו הֲרֵי כָּל נְכָסַי נְתוּנִים לְךָ בְּמַתָּנָה.

12   אָמַר: הֲרֵי הֵם עָלַי חֵרֶם וְאֵינִי אֶלָּא שָׁוֶה בָּם כְּאֶחָי.

1. Rabbi Eliezer's brothers were once plowing in the plain while he was plowing on the mountain.

2. His cow fell over and was maimed.

3. He said to himself: "It is to my benefit that she was maimed."

4. He fled.

5. He went to [the academy of] Rabbi Yochanan b. Zakkai.

6. He ate there clods of earth until his mouth emitted an offensive odor.

7. They went and told R. Yochanan b. Zakkai: "The breath from Eliezer's mouth smells foul."

8. He said to them: "Just as the smell of his mouth is unpleasant for the sake of the Torah, so will the fragrance of his learning be diffused from one end of the world to the other."

9. After some time his father came up to disinherit him.

10. He found him sitting and lecturing with the greatest of the land sitting before him: Ben Tzizit Hakesef, Nikodemon ben Gurion, and Ben Kalba Sabua.

11. Said his father to him: "My son, I came up only to disinherit you; now, however, all my property is given to you as a gift."

12. He answered, "Let it be accursed to me; I will only take an equal share with my brothers."

The final story in this collection deals with the early career of an eminent scholar. Although he will be later known as a great rabbi, the Eliezer we first meet is not a noted sage. Rather, he is a simple country boy discontented with his life. Once again, the author of our tale could have told the story with far greater detail, but as with the other stories in the collection, we are presented instead with a miniature tale that is best understood after careful thought.

Questions

1. Based on what we are told, why might Eliezer be plowing apart from his brothers? What is significant about the difference in location?
   a. What might the plain represent?
   b. What might the mountain represent?

2. A characteristic of the Hebrew original is preserved in the English: the brothers' "plowing in the plain." What might this alliteration symbolize?

3. What is the possible significance of the cow's falling over and becoming maimed?

4. How might Eliezer choose to interpret the occurrence? What are his possible responses?

5. "It is to my benefit that she was maimed." What does he mean by this statement?

6. What are the possible reasons for Eliezer's fleeing? From what—or whom—does he flee?

7. Eliezer goes to the academy of Rabbi Yochanan in Jerusalem. What is significant about his destination?

8. What is noteworthy about Eliezer's diet? Does it teach us something general about Eliezer's character?

9. What is surprising about R. Yochanan's response?

10. Why does the father decide to disinherit his son? Why does he choose to do this act in Jerusalem and not at home?

11. Why are the actual names of the important guests mentioned?

12. Why does the father choose to reverse his decision? What is symbolic about his gift to Eliezer?

13. Based on what has already occurred, how might R. Eliezer have responded to his father's announcement?

14. What is significant about R. Eliezer's decision concerning the money?

The poet William Blake once observed: "Great things are done when men and mountains meet." This may be so, but most of us are not interested in being great. We are happy enough being comfortable. Eliezer's brothers are contented farmers, plowing the plain and living in harmony with one another and with the land. But Eliezer is different. Either out of compulsion or choice, he plows the rocky mountainside, a most trying task. It may reflect his desire to live a life of hardship in order to achieve spiritual heights. Plowing on the mountain is not good farming. But enduring hardship can lead to spiritual riches.

One thing is clear in the brief tableau presented by the narrator: Eliezer is separated from his brothers. Like Joseph in the Bible, he is different from them. He also takes greater risks as a farmer. A cow's becoming injured on the hillside was not unusual, and it easily can be understood as a misfortunate event. A caring Eliezer would respond by helping the cow. Perhaps he does help and our narrator does not see fit to describe this assistance. Instead we are treated to Eliezer's thoughts, which are markedly self-centered. In short, Eliezer sees in the cow's suffering a perfect opportunity to run away.

At this point in the story, Eliezer's plan is not clear. Why is the cow's suffering to his benefit, and why does he choose to run away? Is he running *from* something (a bad job or dysfunctional family) or running *to* something (a life of which he has dreamed)? As we soon discover, he may be "running from," but primarily he is "running to," and his destination is Jerusalem, a city on the top of a mountain. In short, Eliezer trades one mountain for another. And as we will see, his life does not become any easier or more social. But he does begin studying Torah, and this turns out to be both his passion and his genius. Just as the cow "breaks," so he, too, makes a break from his past.

You can take Eliezer out of the farm but you can't take the ascetic out of Eliezer. Just as before, Eliezer takes the hardest, rockiest path he can find. He does not join a community. He remains a loner and does not even permit himself to eat food. It is true that, given Eliezer's having run away from home, his finances are probably not great. Nevertheless, the story suggests that he may be enjoying the deprivation. Perhaps R. Yochanan understands this strange joy; in any case, he chooses not to intervene. Instead, he lets Eliezer continue with his ascetic ways.

The sage understands there is a spiritual benefit to physical suffering, although in general Jewish tradition does not support such suffering. A sustained movement of physical deprivation never developed in Jewish spiritual life. As the Sages used to say: "If there is no flour, there can be no Torah study." Eliezer may be the exception to the rule but, for the rest of the students, the advice is clear: don't try this at home. Having said that, Yochanan acknowledges that the reward for such deprivation will be great spiritual fame.

After some time (we don't know how long), Eliezer's father comes to disinherit him. Why in Jerusalem? Maybe there was an administrative reason. Perhaps the father knew his son was there and wanted to speak with Eliezer or see what he was doing. Maybe his father wanted to humiliate Eliezer. From his perspective, the father had a right to be angry with Eliezer for abandoning his work and leaving his brothers soley responsible for the upkeep of their lands. The narrator is vague regarding the choice of Jerusalem, but the event unfolds with clarity. The father, who turns out to be a man of some wealth, ends up at Rabbi Yochanan's House of Study, along with the great rich men of the time. The fact that their names are mentioned gives an authentic flavor to the story. But they also are important because they are recognizable as rich and famous men, and Eliezer's father certainly would know of them and be impressed by them.

What is most incredible, of course, is that his son should be lecturing. In those times it was the custom for the sage to sit while others stood. For Eliezer to be in this position indicates that he was by then a noted and honored scholar. His father may be impressed by Eliezer's brilliant learning, but more likely he is influenced by the fact that rich men are impressed with his son. The father's values have not changed: money means more to him than scholarship. But when money respects scholarship, so does he. In what must have been an emotional moment, he admits his former plan to disinherit his son and then announces that all his property will be given to Eliezer instead.

Eliezer's response is to reject the gift, if not in total then at least in its majority. He even declares it to be "accursed." Nevertheless, he has also learned something about the need to belong to a family. And so instead of rejecting his share and continuing in his ascetic ways, the older and wiser Eliezer is not above sharing the gift with his brothers. In the end not only has he learned great Torah, he has also learned something about being a genuine human being.

CONCLUSION

Hopefully, the study of these stories has accomplished two things: revealed how the ancient Jewish Sages addressed important issues of character in their day, and offered insights into our own human psyche. Concerning the first issue, I hope to have shown that the Sages were in fact gifted storytellers who often weaved stories notable for their style as well as their substance. The stories in this collection are not filled with many details. We are not told how the characters appeared. We are given no description of the houses or the vistas. The terse style is more Ernest Hemingway than Charles Dickens. Nevertheless, the stories creatively present fine human dramas and offer timely insights into the nature of humanity.

Regarding human nature, based on the stories we studied the following points have been made:

- Torah study can easily be abused by people who use their studies as an excuse to avoid their family responsibilities. The Sages who told these stories condemned such avoidance. They realized that Torah learning without simple human decency is an abomination.

- In life, good process leads to good products. In other words, if we practice kindness and if we observe basic rituals such as keeping the Sabbath, our lives will reflect that goodness. We cannot directly change fate, but we can ensure that God notices righteous living. This is not to say that bad things will not happen to good people. But it does suggest a philosophy for life: do good and let God take care of the rest.
- Finally, a little humility is a good way to avoid trouble in life. Even if we are a well-respected sage or lay person, we should not feel we are doing enough for our families or for the needy in our midst. We can always do more.

I hope this book will inspire those who read it to continue their studies of Jewish stories. The above nine stories only scratch the surface of the tremendous amount of material available. Tales such as those presented here can entertain us and teach us how to be better human beings. Elie Wiesel once said that God created the world because God loves stories. As these tales suggest, through such stories we can be reminded of God's expectations for us, and we can see that creating the world for the sake of stories is not a bad reason at all.

Bibliography

Barkai, Yair. *The Miniature Story* (in Hebrew). Jerusalem: David Schon Institute, 1986.

Braude, William G., trans. *The Book of Legends*. New York: Schocken, 1992.

Cohen, Jonathan. "On the Moral Significance in Teaching an Aggadic Story," *Studies in Jewish Education* vol. 1, ed. Barry Chazan. Jerusalem: Magnes, 1983, pp. 40–50.

Fraenkel, Jonah. "Paranomasia in Aggadic Narratives" *Studies in Hebrew Narrative Art Throughout the Ages,* vol. 27, ed. Joseph Heinemann and Shmuel Werses. Jerusalem: Magnes, 1978, pp. 27–51.

——. *Studies in the Spiritual World of the Aggadic Story* (in Hebrew). Tel Aviv: Hakibbutz Hameuchad, 1981.

Goldberg, Edwin. *Midrash for Beginners*. Northvale, N.J.: Jason Aronson, 1996.

Licht, Chaim. *Ten Legends of the Sages*. Hoboken, N.J.: Ktav, 1991.

Glossary

chevruta: In this style of Jewish traditional study, two people carefully explore the nuances of the text. The word is derived from the Hebrew word for "friendship" or "society."

midrash: The word has two basic meanings. It is both a *process* of interpreting the Bible and a *collection* of classic works that interpret the Bible. Midrash can interpret legal sections of the Bible or narrative sections. The narrative midrash is also called *midrash aggadah* (story midrash).

Midrash *B'reishit Rabbah:* This collection of interpretations on the Book of Genesis was created in Palestine by the ancient rabbis, c. 400 C.E.

Midrash *D'varim Rabbah:* This work of interpretation of the Book of Deuteronomy was composed by rabbis of ancient Palestine, c. 500 C.E.

Midrash *Vayikra Rabbah:* This collection of sermons based on the Book of Leviticus was created in Palestine by the ancient rabbis, c. 500 C.E.

Rashi: Rabbi Solomon ben Isaac (1040–1105) was a leading commentator on the Bible and Talmud. He was born in Troyes, France. His comments are studied by every traditional talmudic student.

Satan: According to the ancient rabbis who created the Talmud and midrash, Satan has two characteristics: he is the personification of the evil urge (see below) that tempts us to evil, and he is the "prosecuting attorney" in the heavenly court. In this latter role, he seeks to prove to God that human beings are not worthy of their blessings.

Talmud (Babylonian and Palestinian): These two lengthy works comprise the essential part of what is called the "oral Torah," the traditions that Moses supposedly received from God on Mount Sinai but which were not written down in the Bible. The core of both works is the Mishnah (collected teachings) of Rabbi Judah the Prince of Palestine (c. 210 C.E.). One commentary (Gemara) to the Mishnah was completed in fifth-century Palestine and is called the Palestinian or Jerusalem Talmud. The other commentary was completed about one hundred years later in Babylon. This second Talmud became more well-known in the Jewish world.

tractate: The word that describes a section of the Talmud. A tractate usually is named for a certain subject matter, such as "blessings" *(B'rachot).*

yetzer hara: The term refers to the evil urge. According to the ancient rabbis, each human being has an evil urge that tempts him or her to do the wrong thing. This urge can be controlled through Torah study and the observance of mitzvot (commandments).